How to Start Over

poems

Stuart Kestenbaum

DEERBROOK EDITIONS

PUBLISHED BY
Deerbrook Editions
P.O. Box 542
Cumberland, ME 04021
www.deerbrookeditions.com
e-catalog: www.issuu.com/deerbrookeditions

FIRST EDITION
© 2019 by Stuart Kestenbaum
All rights reserved
ISBN: 978-0-9600293-4-1

Book design by Jeffrey Haste
Cover art: *The Letter A* by Susan Webster

For Susan

Table of Contents

I

Dust Broom in the Studio   13
Amen   14
Fake News   15
Listening to Stones   16
At Old Orchard Beach   17
Mourner's Prayer   19
Joy   20
Spring Day   21
Laboratory   22
First Light   23
On the Road to Damascus   25

II

Balance   29
Answers   30
Separation Blues   31
Lullaby   32
Blue   33
To Life   34
Intentional   35
Change   36
Civilization   37
Coastline   38
Corporate Lament   39
Learning to Pray   40
Commencement Address   41
Decree   42
Discovering Fame   43
Evening Song   44
Getting Started   46
God Hands Creation Over to Us   47
Harmonic   48
Fair Day   49
Hermit's Dream   50

III

How to Start Over 53
Our Sickness 54
Love Lesson 55
Peace 56
College 57
Tashlich 58
Time Traveler 59
Learning to Hope 60
Self-Improvement Manual 61
Oh, Morning 62
It's Not Always About You 63
Necessity 64
Call Home 65
Harmonize 66
Meditation 67
Alive 68
Solving It 69
Such Stuff as Dreams 70
The Tao of Politics 71
Sleep 72

IV

Becoming a Poet 75
All Dressed Up 77
Last Night I Dreamed I Had My Heart Replaced 79
Awesome 81
Anthem for the Garden State 83
Self 85

Acknowledgments 87

A note on sections II and III. These poems were composed using words given to me by other people. When I was a visiting writer at the Penland School, I asked workshop participants to provide random words and, once I was home, extended the same invitation to friends and family. These words are listed at the end of each poem in alphabetical order. I allowed myself to alter the tense or part of speech, sometimes separating the components of a two-part entry. In a few instances, a cluster of words inspired more than one poem.

In addition to the Penland workshop participants, I am grateful to the following people for supplying me with words: Alan Bray, Akiko Busch, Neil Gershenfeld, Isaac Kestenbaum, Sam Kestenbaum, Liz Lerman, Wesley McNair, Naomi Shihab Nye, Nadya Peek, Bill Roorbach, Betsy Sholl, Susan Webster, Monica Wood, and Malika Ziane—and staff at Northern Light Eastern Maine Medical Center, students at Virginia Commonwealth University, and attendees of the New Hampshire Arts Education Partnership Conference.

I

Dust Broom in the Studio

Yellow nylon bristles
brown with the residue
of dirt, those motes
of dust that pile up
to make the chaos
that always surrounds us.
The ends of the bristles
look like a cross section
of a fiber optic network,
the communication between
floor and dustpan.
O what amazing things
it has swept up:
the luminescent green
wings of a luna moth,
eons old stones
that have traveled
in the grooves of our sneakers,
the inner light
of fluorescent tubes,
the crumpled, the broken, the windblown
things of this material world.
Its handle holds the hands
of all who clean,
all who dream of the empty space
all who are ready to begin again.

Amen

It's easy to ignore the moment we dwell in
the time when we should be our own choir

shouting *amen* to every second that's given us
but we forget and think only of the machinery

that's driving our lives, the idling
engines of our day-to-day-to-day, the endless

tapping on the keyboards. Or else we're waiting
for something better to come along, some

out-of-town engagement better than where we
are now. Life isn't some film we can review again,

it's live theater, and even if we could go back
what's the point? Sitting in the darkened room

with the film ticking along and we reverse
the projector and see ourselves

returning in the car before we've ever left
walking backwards to our house

or leaping out of the water
we thought we were swimming in.

Fake News

I remember what poetry is watching YouTube
when Stephen Colbert begins his monolog with
a joke about the top news of the day, a moth drinks

a tear out of a sleeping bird's eye, he says, showing
a photo to the audience, which laughs when he gives
an "only kidding" look and says I wish I were the bird,

I wish I were the moth instead of someone who had to
pay attention to Donald Trump, and then launches into
the news of the day, but I think these two winged

creatures living symbiotically could have been
the lead story, along with the two boys on old bikes
riding past a house on a quiet street who ask us "are you

moving in?" or the cypress trees that have knees that help
stabilize them in the swamp and breathe during floods.
How much can enter our minds, how often people

say "Look" meaning I'm exasperated can't you hear
what I'm saying to you, not "Look" as in let us all
open our eyes. These are the eyes that are open,

this is the 24/7 news channel, this is the bird
that is sleeping, this is the moth, its wings beating,
its brief life already over by the time you are reading this.

Listening to Stones

Venus de Milo at the Louvre for Bruce Bulger

At first there are so many
people crowded around her

with cameras, smart phones and iPads
that it looks like a press conference,

only Venus isn't taking any questions
from the reporters today, she is risen

above us, and the tourists
below ebb and flow all day

like the ocean around the island
of Milo, where she used to live, where

stones must have life inside them
to make the gestures so human that

even the eyes are watching us.
She isn't timeless for you can see

the passage of centuries in the pockmarks
on her armless torso and her face yet

she survives as we all survive—humans,
gods or stones—in the immutable light,

how still she stays through the busy day
and the silent, cool, star-filled night.

At Old Orchard Beach

Just beyond the steady waves and sandy shore
the arcade with the pinball machines that kids shove
from side to side to try for a replay and Skee-Ball,

a game that always begins with hope
and ends with a cheap toy. Nearby
the painted carousel horses make

their eternal rounds, gaining and losing ground,
brave steeds ridden by small children off
into the unknowable future. We eat

pizza, french fries, fried dough. Just enough
to regret. Off in the distance the remnants
of the great pier that was washed away, the waves

breaking underneath, riding up on the wooden pilings.
We watch our children as they thrill
to all the tacky possibilities and, prodded by them,

toward sunset my brother and I find ourselves
locked in and rising on the roller coaster
overlooking the Atlantic and the now flickering lights

of the food stalls below. We're moving inevitably
and slowly higher before our first descent
when he turns to me and says, "this is just like death,"

and he's right, how when it's your turn
there's no getting away from it, even though we don't
know then that he will die before I will, this

late summer evening when the car drops so fast
on the old wooden frame that our fear can
hardly catch up with us. We leave on wobbly legs.

Back on the ground there's an old man
who guesses your weight, occupation
or age, win or lose, everyone gets a prize.

Mourner's Prayer

September 11, 2014

There is no stopping the sun
in its arc across the sky

how it rises every day, or we turn
toward it, as its light

touches the tops of the trees
or the bedrock by the shore

or the wings of the jets miles above us
as if each day the light

is discovering the world.
The light makes the heat that

makes the water rise up
to become the clouds that

drift one after another over the land.
There are no borders for the clouds

or the wind or the light, all of which
move freely without passports.

Every day the light touches
the broken tar by the shoulders

of the worn-out road, the dusty goldenrod
bowing in the blue air. In the morning

we discover the roadside apples
that, shaken by the wind, have fallen overnight

unpicked, now food for deer, luminescent
and shining back at the sun.

Joy

The asters shake from stem to flower
waiting for the monarchs to alight.

Every butterfly knows that the end
is different from the beginning

and that it is always a part
of a longer story, in which we are always

transformed. When it's time to fly,
you know how, just the way you knew

how to breathe, just the way the air
knew to find its way into your lungs,

the way the geese know when to depart,
the way their wings know how to

speak to the wind, a partnership of feather
and glide, lifting into the blue dream.

Spring Day

The tide empties and fills the cove
where the worm diggers come at low tide
and leave behind the hieroglyphs
of their rakes in the mud.

These etchings fade over time
a scarification of the flat that catches the light
from the west. The sun moves north every day
now entering the window at sunset, aligned

with the panes so that the light is like a beacon
as if the people who built our house
150 years ago were Druids who saw
how everything lines up and we could know

when to plant, when to harvest. As the sun
enters the room, it highlights the scratches
on the plaster, every nick on the wall, cobweb
and drip of paint, a starlet

without makeup, but I've grown used to
seeing our imperfections this way,
bathed in light and washed over every day
the way the tide washes over the digger's marks.

We are here for a while short or long, we are
light and earth, we are what we know
and don't know, we are
old scars and something stirring.

Laboratory

We're always thinking of those hours
of splendor in the grass, the glory

in the flowers and trying not to grieve
as if grieving is bad for us,

not one of those necessary vitamins
for which there must be a required

daily amount as much as there is for
happiness and if you were a scientist

in the laboratory of life, you would be
pouring the sorrow and happiness

back and forth in the test tubes,
heating them together on your

Bunsen burner, hoping to get them
to combine so that we could go beyond

one or the other, go beyond the grief
that is whispering in our ears.

We would have the two together,
the perfect combination, the joy

and sorrow, the call and response,
the wind and the leaves, the sprout and the earth,

the compost and the seed, because everything
needs something else to make it whole,

even the hole needs its own emptiness
the call in the dark, the echo in the light.

First Light

In the beginning, right after
light was summoned forth
God separated the light
from the dark and then one
thing followed the next, the division
of the earth from the heavens,
the water from dry land until

eventually we were here
waking up every day and going to work.
But that wasn't the end of it
with the light and the dark,
because when the light appears
isn't every day the first one?

Those summer mornings of muted fog,
the dazzling clarity of the fall,
the pollen-full air of spring or
the brief winter days when
darkness waits in the wings.
At dawn the landscape begins

to resume its shape before our eyes
and the photographers are out
gathering light like scientists or
like detectives after evidence, trying
to get back to the start of things
when light and dark were brand new

and light began to sing stories
that go by in the blink of an eye,
unless the shutter opens
so we see that moment
that was never here before
and won't be back again.

the fragrant blossom, the shadow
of a man, the tide running out,
the second growth forest transforming itself.
The light writes itself on the dark and the dark
embraces it, the two forces joined
together again, full spectrum holiness.

On the Road to Damascus

after "Damascus" by Elise Ansel

Even people who don't know that they are praying
are praying, are whispering inside from ear to ear
and hearing the rhythm of their own hearts.

Even the people who don't know they are full
of light are full of light, are glowing from
inside their torn coats or tailored suits.

Of course it's always the mumble of every day
that gets our attention. You're driving in your
car listening to the news repeat itself endlessly

or hearing a caller to the talk show say,
can you hear me? I'll take my answer
off the air when suddenly you find yourself on the shoulder

rolled over twice, glass glistening in your hair
like a shattered halo, tree limbs swaying above you.
We are taught to think *get back on the horse* meaning

to push on, but what if the horse is telling you
to stop too? The horse is also full of light.
Look, it says, the world is glowing, the world

is alive. Be kind to me and be kind to yourself.
It may be as simple as that, but you are
stunned, your arms reach for where you once were

but that place doesn't exist anymore, for you have
been thrown out of the everyday into this place
of light. It's no wonder that you were blinded

for three days. You can spend the rest of your life
trying to understand this rogue wave from the unspeakable
darkness, trying to speak the wordless into words.

II

Balance

Don't worry. There's nothing to fear,
the wolf is not at the big oak door

with his red eyes glowing.
History won't be repeating itself

and there's no need to be checking
your inbox looking for love. Love

will find you if you can still imagine it.
For all you know it may arrive as

a delicious absurdity. Mike Meyers,
Amy Schumer, and the Buddha rolled

into one. You know for every upswing
there's a downswing, but, oh!, the ride.

balance, delicious, fear, history, love, Michael Meyers, oak, red, upswing,
wolf

Answers

If I were a scientist, chalk in hand,
I could scribble an ansatz on the board

and wait for my research team to join me
in their white lab coats, applying their

brain power, swaying back and forth
as if praying in a numeric trance.

Or I could be embroidering instead
putting my intelligent hand to work,

each stitch an accretion of my fingers'
growing knowledge.

Whatever system we apply to the problem—
even if out of frustration we resort to dysphemisms

to hide our own insecurities, call ourselves
simpletons instead of seekers—the best way

to get there is to wander all night, to get lost in the thicket
of our souls where the answers are always

all of the above or maybe. There we are at dawn,
in the yellow light, the rain from last night's storm

rising to heaven or filling the reservoirs,
birds chirping today's questions.

accretion, ansatz, apply, dysphemism, embroidered, maybe, morning,
reservoir, swaying, yellow

Separation Blues

Years before China began making the world
in factories and more factories,
I saw a documentary where two men
walked into a bamboo forest
and cut down a tree. So straight and tall,
segmented like our own spines.
They used just a handsaw and knives.
After it fell, they bound it
to another tree with strips made
of its own bark, tightened like a seat belt
for its ride out to become scaffolding
at a construction site or a table in a bedroom.
The ground underfoot must have been like
a velvet cushion since the forest
was so silent in its radiance, just
the saw and the men talking when necessary.
It seemed like something mutual going on:
we borrow, but not too much. A small part
of the forest goes, the rest remains.
Can't we have a little give and take?
However we wish it our life is no
clean slate, there's the spinodal messiness
of what just happened, the hot and cold
running water of our dreams, changed
and changed again but not lost.

bamboo, construction, mutual, radiance, seat belt, slate, spines, spinodal,
velvet

Lullaby

At bedtime think
of the sparrow at dusk
at the end of its

long day of flight
and food, a feverish
life of survival,

think of the ice
crystals building themselves
over the surface of the lake,

transforming into jewels
in the cold silence,
think of the maple in the field,

with its spalted wood,
the irregular lines of decay
that cut and sanded

become beautiful
in the cabinetmaker's hands.
Think of singing softly

to yourself, in the necessary
language, your tongue
your song. Sleep.

bedtime, feverish, jewel, lake, necessary, spalted, sparrow

Blue

Oh my darling, I would love
to sing you a song
backed by my own horn section.
I would love to send you
chocolate and oranges to eat
in the shade of a giant maple,
a tree whose roots are lucky
to be near you.
I would be happy to wash
your rental car or
carve up your pumpkin
with a skill-saw to make
a jack-o-lantern who
would speak on my behalf
declaring nothing but my
love for you. Speak to me!
Tell it to me straight, use
the vernacular, nothing embellished
upon the gold altar of grammar.
Speak to me heart to heart.
I am ready to listen.

car, gold, horn, jack-o-lantern, oranges, roots, skill-saw, vernacular

To Life

Do you know the old chestnut
about the constipated mathematician?

That's the one where he
worked it out with a pencil,

but making a punch line is not
solving a problem,

and the very life of our planet is not
a joke or some academic exercise we're

slogging through, but aqua bogs
so full of life that they can vex us

and also make us want to bow down
before them at the same time.

While we're on our knees shouldn't
we venerate bread dough too, those

yeasty bubbles rising right through
the thick of things and soon enough

it's morning and we are fed
by a mystery just out of the oven.

academic, aqua, bread dough, chestnut, feeding, pencils, planet, venerate, vex

Intentional

Forget about wanderlust,
we've got to be here
for some reason or other
in this crescendo of creativity

that we call evolution.
Aren't we trying to turn
into something less
imperfect, can't we be as wise

as the fruit weighing
down the branch,
such an elegant design to move
the seed along in time?

Or consider the intelligence
of the cut-up starfish,
whose limbs can grow
other bodies out of disaster.

We've all got our burdens,
but why do we always
trot out "heavy" to modify it,
why not think of another

adjective, so that we're not always
trudging into the next day.

Who else but us could have
imagined imagining?

creativity, crescendo, fruit, heavy, intentional, starfish, wanderlust

Change

The cardinal started out regal, opulent,
next in line to the Pope but reaching

North America turned into a bird pausing
on a branch to consider its fate before

becoming a baseball player standing
on the berm of the pitcher's mound

in St. Louis, undistracted by fans
and their air horns, pausing to look into

the catcher signaling the next pitch
in the fading afternoon light.

Baseball is all about statistics and probability,
but isn't that just another way to think about

chance and fate, those cumulants and moments
we can analyze forever, raw data turned

into something that might fly: bird or
ball or saint, who wouldn't be surprised

to have the agency to be in mid-air
headed heavenward?

afternoon, agency, air horn, berm, cardinal, change, cumulants, pausing,
raw, surprised

Civilization

We could be standing sentry over
Constantinople or Byzantium before that.
It's a remarkable vista,
looking at the long march of history,
how technology propels us forward
and how conscientious all of our would-be
leaders want to appear. They are spackling
walls with new slogans, looking for
the momentum of sincerity.
That's an impossibility, as unnatural as
fluorescent lighting. We want our lives
to crackle with what isn't frivolous.
We want to build domes
that will be shining in the sun
We want the horizon to be ours.

conscientious, Constantinople, crackle, fluorescent, frivolous, horizon,
impossibility, momentum, sentry, sincerity, technology, vista

Coastline

Above the gray the gulls
cry in their own alphabet.

Is it danger they're talking about
or just birds being flippant,

reminding us they've been following
us, hovering behind fishing boats,

circling the dumps, and their cry passes
from generation to generation.

If it's a song, it's a stilted one:
no melody really

just a way to regularize want.
They're looking for the next

opportunity, the table set,
each morsel a sweetener

of existence. Brief lives
for us all, lifted by wind

holding ourselves steady
in the Sabbath of the sky.

alphabet, danger, flippant, gray, regularize, Sabbath, stilted, sweetener, table

Corporate Lament

May we all be forgiven
for clawing our way,
circumventing rules, convincing

ourselves that no means
yes, double-dipping
into our own deceit, understanding

the texture of greed.
We wake to find we are
someone we wouldn't know

worried for no apparent reason.
There must be more sparkle than this.
Life is more than popping the bottle cap

and having another cold one.
Life isn't a cheap date between
the solution and the problem.

There must be more than
spinning the wheel of fortune
and hoping for the best.

*bottle cap, cheap date, circumvent, claw, disguised, double-dip, forgiven,
no, sparkle, textured, wheels, worried*

Learning to Pray

We want the world to bedazzle us,
so we tie our hammock ropes to two sturdy
spruce trees and watch the galloping
clouds overhead. We're waiting for
God to whisper in our ears, or if we're shy,
we'll call it the universe, and ask it
to send a sign. But the sign is in us
when we're ready to take our own shovels
dig deep and deeply at the same time.
It's not about success or failure.
It's like a river: every meander is meant
to be, and the silt left after a flood
is the miracle in which we plant our seeds.

bedazzle, failure, hammock ropes, river, shovel, silt, tree, whisper

Commencement Address

Don't worry about your
reputation and don't expect
beams of light to be guiding
your path each step of the way.

Learn from your accidents.
Learn not to box yourself in.
Learn to work the kinks out.
Learn how things grow.

While you're out looking for serenity,
run for governor.
While you're on the campaign trail
plant willows along the riverbank.

Watch how they stop erosion.
Watch how the leaves gather light and breathe.
Listen to the people.
Plant silence in the ground.

accident, beam, box, governor, kink, reputation, serenity, willow leaves

Decree

Let there be equality in every marriage
and let love emulate Newtonian physics
falling down to earth from the heavens
so that we will understand that a pound of love

drops at the same rate as a pound of iron
or a pound of feathers, only when love lands
it breaks into slivers of hope. Let the dogs
roll in the shards and begin to trot deliriously

in search of crusts of pizza and cupcake wrappers
and swim to the land of dead things to roll in
for hope is eternal in all our hearts
animals and humans alike. And while

we're at it, let's gather up the love
and put it in loose-leaf binders and page
through what was. Let *was* become *is*.
Let our hearts learn to be.

*cupcake, delirium, dog, emulate, evoke, loose leaf, marriage equality, New-
tonian, pizza, sliver, swim*

Discovering Fame

Back when there were stage doors
you were standing outside one in the alley,

smoking a last cigarette waiting
to appear on Oprah.

The smoke flowed through your body
and you exhaled the perfect "o"s

which traveled down the narrow space
between the brick walls. You were

passing time, wondering what
the two of you would be talking about

what she could possibly want to know about
your tangled unseen life

the intimacy of recovery
or the scent of the money you were making.

Remember that day? You were collecting yourself,
waiting to serve up your memories before

a national TV audience, making logarithmic
calculations about your soul's journey

into the bright lights.

*discovery, flow, intimacy, logarithmic, memory, money(making), Oprah,
passing, perfection, recovery collecting, scent, serve, smoking unseen, talk-
ing, tangled, time, travel*

Evening Song

At first you can't hear
the melody, your mind

being too busy replaying
the vicissitudes of every day

with its petty deceits.
Does it feel

that you are
betrothed to a burden?

Toward evening you walk
into your field to see

the larvae of weevils
ready to burrow into

everything you've planted.
Time to blame someone else,

caterwaul against confusion.
And then you hear them,

the spring peepers in the pond, emerging
from some salubrious laboratory

of life, to sing, if not a hymn of happiness
then at least a raucous tune

made of water and light.
Why not laugh?

How much more
do you need?

betrothed, burden, caterwaul, deceit, laugh, melody, peepers, salubrious, vicissitudes, weevil

Getting Started

This morning I open Pandora's box
and find that it is full of cat videos

from the internet and while I have
a great sensitivity to animals, I know

I want a deeper message, not a relic
from the past, but something that can

revive me. I don't want to devour
more crispy snacks, as much as

I love Pringles. I'm after that thing
that will bloom. Let's go outside.

There's a road that curves
and curves again, moving

through all kinds of weather
real and imagined.

bloom, cats, crisp, Pandora, relic, revive, road, sensitivity, snacks

God Hands Creation Over to Us

We thought we could be as bodacious
as the eternal one, understanding
the alchemy of ammonia, lightning,
and spirit. Then we were like the dog
that finally catches the car, that junction where
circumstances beyond our control
were suddenly under ours.
How overwhelming to get
a handle on metamorphosis,
watching all those butterflies
drifting off in the wind on our first day
on the job, becoming one thing after another.
And then there were the starfish:
cut the arms off and each one grows
into another being. We were
assembly line workers who couldn't
keep up with the conveyor belt.
We had to take a deep breath
in this heaving world.
Before it had been enough
to make glass out of sand and fire,
but how not to turn out slipshod work
now that everything was up to us?
Then the snow began.
We looked up to make sure
each flake was different,
the sky turned from blue to black, the snow
ticking on the fallen leaves,
landing in the pond,
making small ripples everywhere.

alchemy, bodacious, butterflies, glass, heaving, junction, ripples, slipshod,
snowflake, starfish

Harmonic

There you were, trying to be cogent
about climate change, telling yourself
that we had to think of our world
as an island. You can see it now:
the ocean slapping against the stone,
then lichen, sweet grass, the birch trees
standing between earth and heaven
singing from roots to branches.
After a lifetime of milling about,
you were at the center
of things. It was way past the time
to be romantic, or even lament
that the world was filled with cement
and that the monarchy of greed had
taken over what you loved. Were you
beyond all that? You were
in the presence of breath, a moment
when you became your own
reptilian mind, warming
in the sun, tongue flicking
into the divine air, all the cells learning
to work together as one.

birch, cement, climate change, cogent, harmonic, island, milled, moment,
monarchy, presence, reptilian, romantic, stone, sweet

Fair Day

It's hard to know what to eat next,
the offerings of each booth calling
to a specialized part of your stomach:

the French fries and fried dough
strawberry short cake,
sausage with green peppers and onions

and don't forget the deep-fried Oreos.
In this radius of your desire, between
gorging and wanting to win

a big prize, a stuffed animal almost too big
to wrap your arms around,
you understand what bliss is.

It's the growing blue dusk, pulsing like a scrim
as the lights of the thrill rides grow brighter,
the sheep dogs, never easygoing,

finally done herding for the day,
it's the barn swallows swooping,
devouring more insects than you can imagine.

barn swallow, bliss, booth, deep-fried Oreo, easygoing, radius

Hermit's Dream

Living on the mountaintop, I missed
coffee and bacon at first—who doesn't?
and later began to dream of simple things like
applesauce and noodles, since I was living
on air. Passion takes many forms, my
master had always stressed. Look for patterns
he said. Being and non-being are strange
bedfellows. One day anxiety left, drifting
off and settling in a rock cleft far below.
When the light was right, I could watch
its silhouette moving wildly.
I learned the names of my fears
and put them in a basket. Each day I would
climb up the ledges, remembering who I
had been, feeling like a marsupial carrying
all those personalities in my pouch.
Then there was nothing, but it's not what we
fear. No rigor mortis. I was alive and
dancing in this immense nothing that
is everything. Stoics were laughing. Birds
were singing. First morning.

*anxiety, applesauce, bacon, basket, bedfellows, cleft, immensely, marsu-
pial, mountain, noodle, passion, pattern, rigor mortis, silhouette, stoicism,
stressed*

III

How to Start Over

We knew that things were deteriorating.
Gothic houses collapsing, sharks patrolling the lagoons,
the born-again ministers warning of an immediate conflagration.
All the flights to paradise had been cancelled and even
pinhole cameras weren't letting light in.
It got to be so bad we didn't want to listen to the news anymore,
where all we were doing was gawking at someone else's trouble.
It wasn't worth the effort. Where was the satisfaction we longed for?
We couldn't sleep so would spend all night watching the full moon's
beams cement themselves to the silky water and travel for miles
on the waves. Someone was rowing along the shore,
and in the silver light the evergreens were shaking slightly.
At the edge of the forest the thistles
were attaching themselves to the fur of animals.
What serendipity to hitch a ride to your future.

cement, conflagration, deteriorating, evergreen, flight, gawk, moonbeam,
pinhole camera, row, satisfaction, serendipity, sharks, silky, sleep, thistle,
worth

Our Sickness

Who doesn't know that we are lost,
that we have forgotten, if we ever did
know, how to balance. The doctors,

who should be prescribing rest,
are telling us that this is auxesis
that our cells are growing without dividing

as if we can't become anything different
than what we are. These aren't some
sniffles we're talking about,

this is the aggregate of our own darkness
even though everyday people in Ramallah
want nothing more than to eat dinner

with their families, even though off
the coast of Iceland the cod are ready
with their millions of eggs, even though

July wants to be a simple month,
school's out, humidity lifting,
a boy tossing a baseball in the air.

*aggregate, auxetic, balance, forgotten, Iceland, July, lifting, Ramallah, rest,
sniffles*

54

Love Lesson

When you find your sweetheart
sitting under the arbor, the pollen
heavy in the air, resist temptation:
don't transfer all your insecurities
onto her, and don't make your life
an exercise in idolatry, worshipping
beyond belief. We've all been down
those avenues before. Food may
be the way to the heart. Insert
fragrant cloves into oranges or make
her chocolate. Melt it in the oven
and slide the spatula beneath
as if you're slipping into that
once hot now cooling space
where love evolves,
where the kerf of your emptiness
fits perfectly with her
expanding soul you will be
sororal and sexual at once
two tongues, one language.

arbor, avenue, chocolate, clove, idolatry, kerf, sororal, spatula, sweetheart, transfer

Peace

Please, is there no way we can visit
each other anymore, is there nothing
familiar between us, as in couldn't we be
a family that decided it should
have dinner together and talk about
small things that make us smile.
The world echoes: the rifle shots
from a bell tower, the call to prayer
from a minaret, everywhere crowds
singing national anthems, our own
music through the ear-buds. Our fears
and hopes circling one another
as these sounds pass through the thalamus
into our brains and we don't know
what to make of it. Our hearts
understand there is nowhere left to go
and our souls are growing colder.
Couldn't we join together, become
eutectic, stay liquid, when,
left alone, each of us would freeze.
Let's come in out of the cold
join our spirits in a cocoon we spin
together. What effort to break out,
changed, into the blue day. Imagination
drying its wings and getting ready to fly.

*blue, cocoon, effort/effortful, eutectic, familiar, minaret, please, rifle, thala-
mus, visit*

College

It was getting pretty
soporific in the lecture hall
if you know what I mean,
one of those early afternoons
when you would much rather be
sitting on the porch,
watching loosestrife
sway in a meadow, the nestlings
already flown. Instead you want
to rub your eyes raw
or put ointment in
to keep them open
attach jumper cables to the terminals
of your mind, until the professor
starts talking about thixotropic
compounds and takes out
the corn starch and water mixture
to make her point, how it begins
to ooze through those intellectual fingers,
transformed and flowing,
the way you imagine life should be:
an angel sitting on one side of you
your young dog on the other,
both paying attention
and neither taking notes.

dog, loosestrife, nestlings, ointment, porch, soporific, terminals, thixotropic

Tashlich

*A ritual Jews observe during Rosh Hashanah (the New Year) of casting
off the sins of the old year by tossing bread into moving water.*

You might be standing
at a railing
overlooking the Hudson
watching tugboats
at work, or creekside
in the woods where
it is quiet enough
to perceive the life
of small birds,
or lost in the fog
and deep tides on Cobscook Bay.
Wherever you are
in this entanglement
of life and death,
wondering if you've
been a sluggard
all year, pondering why your
life isn't like a movie
where George Clooney,
with gray hair that always
looks good, figures it all out.
You can feel the weight
of every day on your plate,
and want the water
to swallow it
with everything else that
hasn't gone right, want
to feel something uplifting
as you toss out your bread
into this transmissivity of today,
where light and dark meet
and the water finds its way.

*Cobscook, creekside, entanglement, fog, George Clooney, plate, sluggard,
transmissivity, uplifting, weight*

Time Traveler

We understand the benefits
of being alive and are always hoping
that time won't run out for us
as it did for the elms. Remember their
graceful limbs lining all the streets
of your ideal town? But that moment
is gone, as irretrievable as yesterday's
light that was warming the lizard
on the desert rock, that was touching
the dense tops of the sedges nestled
in the ledge along the shore that was
shining on your face as you ate your
bowl of lentils in high afternoon sun.
Don't worry we don't have to become
trans-temporal, for here comes today's light
to touch us again for the first time
particles and waves, call and response.

benefits, elm, irretrievable, lentils, light, lizard, runout, sedge,
trans-temporal, underneath

Learning to Hope

We all want to root for the underdog
not give way to despair, as if it's
us too picking ourselves off the ground
covered in mud. There will always be

trouble, always be banging your hand
against your forehead with what you
have forgotten to do, always the careless
cut from the razor that bleeds more

than you remember. Use the styptic pencil
to stanch the flow. There is no operator's
manual, no secret envelope with the answer,
but there is your own ingenious spirit.

Be the maple tree that invents the samara,
how gracefully it spins, moving purposefully
through a wind not of its own making, to
become itself again in more distant soil.

despair, envelope, forehead, mud, samara, styptic, trouble, underdog

Self-Improvement Manual

Sometimes joy is camouflaged, hiding
in plain sight while you are busy composing
cover letters or filling out taxes, or frantically
reaching into the pocket of your trousers

for your wallet, hoping it's not being emptied
by someone on the train you just left.
That train might be moving down the track
heading toward the vanishing point,

but what if life isn't linear, moving from a baby's
first breath to the last rattle of your time here.
Perhaps you will find yourself slowly inhaling
a holy breath, the one you are exhaling now.

Then you'll know that it's time to fire
the inner management consultant
who tells you a tiger can't change its stripes.
They are, after all, your stripes.

baby's breath, camouflage, empty, joy, letter, slowly, striped, trousers

Oh, Morning

It's no wonder you feel contrary in the morning,
your spirit still half asleep as the day is forming
and you still living in the cloudforest of your dreams
where every green tuft and gnarled tree
connect seamlessly. And then the jolt of morning news
with the latest study linking fill-in-the-blank
with death or at least the blues.
This isn't to say that you don't want
to face reality, for you understand
that there is no free ride and each of us
must do what we can to find
what we've lost, repair what we can.
You're willing to lace up your boots
and get your hide to work,
but you need to turn up the music
hear a songstress who finds the ancient melody
that floats in the air and is gone.

boots, cloudforest, contrary, death, free, link, songstress, tuft

It's Not Always About You

Who isn't afraid of failure? Who doesn't
think the world is whispering
behind their backs. Every day you're
ready to take a shovel and dig
your own grave, or at least a hole
you can crawl into. How about you
stretch some hammock ropes across
that place where you're planning to
sleep forever, tie it to two trees of knowledge
and begin to be bedazzled by the sky,
by the river of life that flows through
you, by the silt that makes
a delta of dreams, a fertile crescent,
a landscape for planting those seeds
that have no names.

bedazzle, failure, hammock ropes, river, shovel, silt, tree, whisper

Necessity

Do whatever is most necessary:
If you have a fever
fill the tub with ice.
If you're at a lake
take off your clothes
and dive under the surface
to the quiet space where
your pulse beats in your ear.
If the sparrow flies into the window
thinking the reflection is another forest,
put it in a dark space until
it comes to its winged senses.
If you find the spalted maple
blown down in a storm,
carve a bowl so that the dark lines of decay
become as beautiful as jewels.
If it's bedtime say your prayers.
What have you got to lose?

bedtime, fever, ice, jewels, lake, necessary, spalted, sparrow

Call Home

I don't suppose we should lament
the decline of the telephone booth,
the one where Superman would do his quick change
or the lonely one teenagers could pelt with eggs
or the one in hot sun of the gas station
at the edge of the farm field, insects whining
and the barn swallows diving like lyrical jet pilots
while your engine overheated.
Or maybe you'd just finished a bag of deep-fried Oreos
at the fair too sick to walk so called home for a ride.
There are so many other things to
worry about in the radius of our caring,
in our search for bliss. Why worry about this
box of light on a dark night? Why not be
easy-going and let the past pass and not search
the coin return to see if there's enough change
to make a call that matters.

barn swallow, bliss, booth, care, deep-fried Oreo, easy-going, radius,
telephone

Harmonize

It's not like you spent
your whole life swimming
against the current, watching
the moon shine on the water as you tried

to hold your own. But you knew
that your life was upside down,
like a camera obscura, that
there must be something you

should embrace, do something
daring like put your heart
on a kite and let it rise in the sky.
It's easy enough to doodle aimlessly,

exclaim with your whole being that you
are a thief, that you stole the pie from
the windowsill of the farmhouse
and ran into the cornfield to celebrate.

Don't be so hard on yourself. The world
goes on without you, the rose blossoms,
the cardinal sings, water
rises to heaven every day.

being, camera, corn, daring, doing, doodle, embracing, exclaiming, harmo-
nizing, kite, moonshine, pie, rose, swimming, thief

Meditation

When the rhubarb emerges from the ground
just about the time you've forgotten
that there can even be a spring.
When the milkweed becomes airborne,

drifting in the harsh November light,
you remember once again that everything
changes, moves, is born, and dies.
It's no heresy to say that when we

are gone we are gone. Gone where?
You might be tempted to call this pondering
navel gazing, as in staring at your belly button,
but who wouldn't want to stare there

at the scarred end of the umbilical cord
that brought us here. This lifeline of all lifelines,
where our cells went about their work
in the laboratory of the unnameable.

belly button, change, everything, forgotten, heresy, light, milkweed,
rhubarb

Alive

No use to mope, dawdle,
tarry or otherwise try to
slow things down like a highway

worker in a chartreuse safety vest
for by now you know
deep in the muscle of your heart

that your life isn't about nothing,
even if you don't know what
the something is.

Seek it out on the store shelves
and don't chicken out on this
journey, for your feral soul

is alive rooting things
out. While you're daydreaming
it's moving in the old fields at dusk

the crabapple blossoms, the first
to come and the first to go,
dropping like pink snow.

chartreuse, chicken, crabapple, feral, mope, muscle, nothing, store

Solving It

If you're a detective, then the world is a stakeout
and nothing is a frill, for every oblique
reference could help you crack the case.

Even when you dream, your third eye
is looking out for things that aren't cricket.
You're not doing things by the book,

but you do keep your own journal made of silence.
You like the night the best, and grow nostalgic
for the flashing lights of the patrol cars, and chalk

outlines on the street. High above the crimes
the lights are attracting swarms of moths, the pale
green luna or the spotted leopard, each flying

like an Icarus of the shadow side while you're
trying to take care of earthly business beneath,
perpetually puzzled but never without a clue.

beneath, cricket, dreams, frill, leopard moth, oblique, silence, stakeout

Such Stuff as Dreams

Silence is what dreams are made on.
Always the silence first, no frills,
just the emptiness. No need to stakeout

the place waiting for images to arrive
from the other world for everything
you need lives within, as if you've

made a bequest to yourself: your flying
self, your running but getting nowhere self,
your weeping self. No wonder

you dream that you are a cricket
with no voice, and discover
you can rub your legs together,

another signal that your body and soul
are one. And while you're playing
the musical saw of your spirit, you see

the leopard moth on its oblique night flight,
living its brief black and white life
with great purpose and no running lights.

bequeath, cricket, dreams, frill, leopard moth, oblique, silence, stakeout

The Tao of Politics

After the election the governor
declared her new platform
to be serenity. Don't box
yourself in, she said. Everything
should be flowing.
Move the same way
that the river moves,
working all the kinks out
with graceful necessity.
She wasn't in it to build her reputation,
for she knew leading was using
knowledge and intuition to manage
chance and accidents.
It was November and the willows
along the banks were shedding
yellow leaves into the river
like so many pages or receipts.
Probably more a receipt
than a page for we've all
run up our own bills, and here they are,
landing on the water's dark surface,
each a tiny boat glowing
in the beams of autumnal light.

accident, beam, box, governor, kink, reputation, serenity, willow leaves

Sleep

This is the bedtime
of your imagined childhood,
the cabin window is open
and you can hear the lake,
you can smell the fresh water.
Today's blinding jewels
of sunlight on the surface
are gone.
In this growing dark
perhaps the moon will rise,
a loon will call out
and another will call back.
A sparrow appears at the window,
such a small spirit, it's as if
your soul is connected
to the night. And isn't it?
Aren't we joined one thing to the other
like the ice crystals that make
their way over the surface,
or how fungus grows in spalted wood,
the black lines manifesting the microscopic?
It's your life, dream
whatever is necessary.

bedtime, fever, ice, jewels, lake, necessary, spalted, sparrow

IV

Becoming a Poet

That first moment came without pen
or notebook in hand on a drive
down the Garden State Parkway
the section near Perth Amboy where
the traffic is heavy and the air is too,
where the little Dutch Boy who back
in ancient history must have founded
his own paint company, is holding
his brush up on a billboard.
My father is driving the white-finned
Buick Electra and I say "the air
smells like Vaseline" to which he says
"you should write that down,
that's what poets do" and from that moment on
I became a poet, not to say I began
to write after that but that was when
the thought entered my head, there
with the Dutch Boy high on the billboard
and the rumble of station wagons and trucks
and off in the distance the Atlantic making
a faint breaking sound of waves against
the sand of the Jersey shore, and farther off
the Statue of Liberty holding its beacon.
The radio is playing and the beauty
of the radio in the car, particularly to young poets,
is that it joins together time and space,
motion and distance and when the song
comes on, the one you have to hear,
that's the only moment that exists,
when the voices as if by some miracle—and isn't
a radio wave a miracle masquerading as science—
when this wave hits your car and you
are awash in rhythm and meaning
and there, that's the poem and that's why

poets sometimes stand there attentive,
because the air is sending messages
whether it's the odor of refineries, the radio waves
or the waves of light emanating from
the very beginning of time or even before
time before light itself, when light
and darkness were one, this is all filling
this day in which the Dutch Boy is applying
a layer of whitewash and the very air is full
of this essence, just waiting to be deciphered.
To swim in this bath of light and dark,
to stroke right through time back to the beginning
or into the future. Who needs a notebook anyway?
Because if it's not made note of, then it slips by,
like meteors at night in the thin air,
a quick flash and gone.

All Dressed Up

They say it was JFK who killed off the hat because
he didn't wear one at his inauguration and maybe
if we look backward we can say that was the beginning
of the end of formality. First the hat, then the white gloves,
then the RSVP, then the thank you note,
then pretty much everything was gone
and eventually you're wearing your sweat suit to the airport.
It's a good thing pilots still dress up because
there is something about a human in uniform,
something about the awkward formality as if the tie
and hat make it possible for you to fly the plane.
But even our soldiers have gone informal in combat fatigues.
In Bangor you can still see hundreds of troops
in desert sand camouflage disembarking
on their way to or from Iraq or Afghanistan.
How that uniform makes things uniform,
man, woman, tall, short, with the names
over the top of the front pocket. We're looking
at the faces of America, glad to be home or fearful
to be going away. They stand outside the airport
smoking cigarettes, making phone calls home.
Each face, each name with a family and each
and everyone of us wanting only to say
"It's going to be okay" as if this is a mantra,
but like any mantra, lots of things begin
to insert themselves into the okay, the rest
of the world being not okay, the rest of the world burning,
which is not the apocalypse, because the world
has been burning ever since the gates to Eden
slammed shut and we heard the sound of the lock engaging.
We imagine the worst but hope for the best,
which is why you want to get dressed up just a little.
Go ahead, put a hat on, wear something
that might make you smile. It's not to say that the hat

will change the world or a tie will either, but there's something
so poignant about looking at yourself in the mirror
as you adjust things just so—millions of years of evolution,
twenty years of school, a pinch of religion, a few
tablespoons of laws and there you are. It's not as if
you've earned this place in the world exactly, but you're here.
You know that it's time to go to work, putting
one foot in front of the other, greeting each day
like someone walking out of the shelter,
like someone emerging from the trenches,
the mute black smoke of destruction
already drifting off in the blue dome of heaven.

Last Night I Dreamed I Had My Heart Replaced

But in the dream I didn't consider the before or after,
didn't think of the surgeons with their scalpels making
the cuts and taking the glistening muscle
which continued for a few beats on its own,
like the cartoon character that's run off the cliff
his legs still moving in thin air.
So there my heart was in that same thin air,
taking in the world for the first time, this loyal pump,
this blue-collar grunt in the engine room of my life
out for the first time, out on its own.
What would a lonely heart like this do?
Go for a walk down the street, the light shining
through the pale green leaves of late May,
whistling so it won't feel so alone, or maybe
just go to the coffee shop, sit at an outside table,
always feeling its beat, its life devoted to rhythm.
In that way the heart might be like a drummer,
a drummer like Ringo Starr, never flashy, always
with a good back-beat, and hearing the rhythm
everywhere: in engines, in wind, in the whir of a fan,
in the rotation of tires on the road. Lonely always
modifies heart, an adjective that clings like last night's
bad dream. Can we sever lonely from heart
with the precision of a surgeon, cut it
and go find a new adjective to walk alongside it,
and let's cut courageous and broken too and then
we can suture ambiguous or complicated in there.
The beat is always with us, the heart with its chambers
holding not secrets but history, not just the French
fries and kale you've eaten, but the first spring
of your life when you realized that everything
was being reborn, if not in your heart well then all around you,
the smallest flowers of the big trees, the daffodils
pushing through the ground, the whole world

a green blush driven by you-know-who or
maybe you-don't-know-who. It doesn't really matter
who's driving, it's the drive that counts,
the impulse before words, the verb before nouns,
the action before the wisdom if indeed
there is any wisdom or perhaps the wisdom
is in the action. The birds know this
and their wings know it too: the beat, the glide,
the turning in unison and quickly back again.

Awesome

What is it that takes your breath away?
What is the small gasp that poets want to hear
at the end of a poem, the little intake of breath,
as if the other breath, the old air that you
were holding inside, had suddenly disappeared
and you needed to fill your lungs with wonder?
There is so much around us that could make us gasp,
if we were to ponder our small marble of a planet
how much space there is, not just
between our star and the next, but between
every molecule and atom on earth, which to me
is not an empirical demonstration of how things
go together but a mystical look at what's between us,
this near and far space we swim in,
this distance even now between each word,
this full spectrum of light that's flooding our world
in ways that our eyes can't see. When we thought
we were at the center of everything, did that
make us happier? Harder to think
about everything expanding, like dots
on the inflating balloon, farther and farther apart,
as we move out from the first magnificent explosion.
Even with all this spinning and moving, even
with all this awe, too much awe to hold
in the modest hard drives of our heads, we want
to take a break from it. Take a break and have
a cup of coffee while we sit in the sun,
the air full of the sound of returning birds,
the water from the rivulets of the forest
full of last year's leaves, the slight trickle of today,
the black flies hatching, the air full of swarms,
the dogs ready to roll in something dead.
What could be better, Einstein sitting
in the chair next to you, tuning up his fiddle,

loving the holiness of sound, the unknowable
vibration that makes the music. He sits back,
body of the violin under his chin.
He's just an OK player, but it doesn't matter.
He draws the bow and air carries wave after wave
of melody, mixing with the waves of light,
which are not only waves, but particles too,
the way we are all more than one thing that's
bundled into what makes our lives. Just yesterday
we were laughing while we were worried about dying
and today we were remembering melodies
we couldn't sing and starting the car, the spark
and gas—the energy, which once was and always will be,
moving with friction down the blacktop and into the light.

Anthem for the Garden State

Home is the place where our bones are fabricated,
the plant where we are assembled, which is why
the first images of *The Sopranos* give me chills,
not because violent people are going to do
violent things to one another, but because of the way
Tony reaches for the New Jersey Turnpike ticket, the way the many
exits could take you to unknown territories in Elizabeth or Bayonne,
and the way that the highways and bridges heading
to New York City have been built over the Meadowlands.
The water flows through the beautiful marsh grass,
past the cheers of the football fans at Giants Stadium,
as if they are rooting for Nature itself, and drains into Newark Bay.
Farther south, the waves are crashing against the shore
at Sandy Hook and Manasquan and to the north,
the Passaic River is flowing past Paterson,
as William Carlos Williams watches, writing
small poems on his prescription pads. On the Turnpike
Walt Whitman and Joyce Kilmer are at the rest stops
that the State has named for them, dreaming
of the sweet corn and the tomatoes in the late summer fields.
Meanwhile the tractor trailers are blowing past the landscape
of house next to house next to house next to house
that makes the woods and open fields seem like a miracle,
and we who were born there know not to laugh
at the Garden State, because it just got here earlier
than the rest of the country, and learned about paving,
and four-lanes and six-lanes and eight-lanes and sixteen-lanes.
We are all driving in the same direction
and Nature is commuting to work like the rest of us,
those wild seeds that find a way into the cracks
of the highway embankments that were painted green
to look like grass. Soon they will be breaking through,
and the many generations will be carried by wind and birds,
trying to make everything a field again.

Dr. Williams has his stethoscope on,
he has placed it on the heart of the abused landscape,
intently listening for a pulse, and he hears a steady beating.
He is jubilant and begins dancing, dancing
for each small seed that has settled down, each small seed
that has exited the highway, that has made it
over the Hudson, over Kittatinny Mountain,
that has floated down the Delaware, past where
General Washington crossed the river,
past where the fields flood in spring
and the buds redden in the morning sun.

Self

The full moon setting
over the frozen cove

is a discovery a surprise
and even though science

could predict it, it can't
anticipate seeing as if

for the first time
the pale white light

again so round so
close as if it called

to you with a "psst"
you I mean you

Acknowledgments

I am grateful to the publications and organizations that first brought out some of the poems in *How to Start Over*.

The Maine Review: "Hermit's Dream," "Decree," "Love Lesson"

Deep Water (*Maine Sunday Telegram*): "Evening Song," "How to Start Over," "Civilization"

In Verse: Maine Places and People (*Lewiston Sun Journal*): "Listening to Stones," "Laboratory"

Ripple Effect: "Tashlich"

Bates College Gallery of Art: "First Light"

Portland Museum of Art/*Beloit Poetry Journal*: "On the Road to Damascus"

Thanks to the Penland School of Crafts and Pocosin Arts School of Fine Craft for providing time and space to work on these poems, and to Betsy Sholl for her careful reading of the manuscript.

About the author

Stuart Kestenbaum is the author of four previous collections of poems, *Pilgrimage* (Coyote Love Press), *House of Thanksgiving, Prayers and Run-on Sentences,* and *Only Now* (all Deerbrook Editions), and a collection of essays, *The View from Here* (Brynmorgen Press). The director of Haystack Mountain School of Crafts from 1988 until 2015, he has written and spoken widely on craft making and creativity. He was appointed Maine's poet laureate in 2016.